Holidays

Passover

by R.J. Bailey

Bullfrog Books

Ideas for Parents and Teachers

Bullfrog Books let children practice reading informational text at the earliest reading levels. Repetition, familiar words, and photo labels support early readers.

Before Reading
- Discuss the cover photo. What does it tell them?
- Look at the picture glossary together. Read and discuss the words.

Read the Book
- "Walk" through the book and look at the photos. Let the child ask questions. Point out the photo labels.
- Read the book to the child, or have him or her read independently.

After Reading
- Prompt the child to think more. Ask: Does your family celebrate Passover? What sorts of things do you see when it's Passover?

Bullfrog Books are published by Jump!
5357 Penn Avenue South
Minneapolis, MN 55419
www.jumplibrary.com

Library of Congress Cataloging-in-Publication Data

Names: Bailey, R.J., author.
Title: Passover / by R.J. Bailey.
Description: Minneapolis, Minnesota: Jump!, [2016]
Series: Holidays | Includes index.
"K to grade 3, ages 5–8"—ECIP data view.
Identifiers: LCCN 2016008096 (print)
LCCN 2016008544 (ebook)
ISBN 9781620313565 (hard cover: alk. paper)
ISBN 9781624964039 (e-book)
Subjects: LCSH: Passover—Juvenile literature.
Classification: LCC BM695.P3 B235 2016 (print)
LCC BM695.P3 (ebook) | DDC 296.4/37—dc23
LC record available at http://lccn.loc.gov/2016008096

Editor: Kirsten Chang
Series Designer: Ellen Huber
Book Designer: Michelle Sonnek
Photo Researchers: Kirsten Chang & Michelle Sonnek

Photo Credits: All photos by Shutterstock except:
Adobe Stock, cover; Alamy, 4, 10, 19, 20–21, 23ml;
Getty, 3; iStock, 1, 6–7, 22; Superstock, 8–9, 23br.

Printed in the United States of America at Corporate Graphics in North Mankato, Minnesota.

Table of Contents

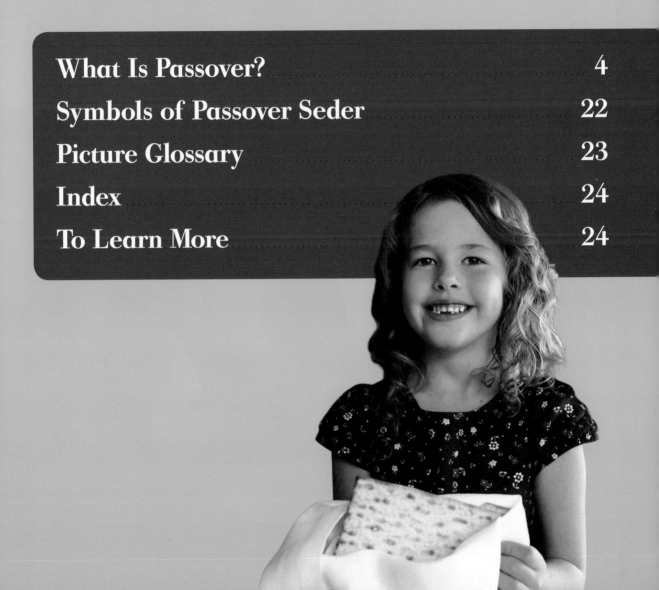

What Is Passover?

Passover is a Jewish holiday.

It is in spring.
It lasts eight days.

What do we celebrate?

We are free!

Jews were once slaves.

They lived in Egypt.

But God sent trouble to the land.

The king was scared.

He let them go.

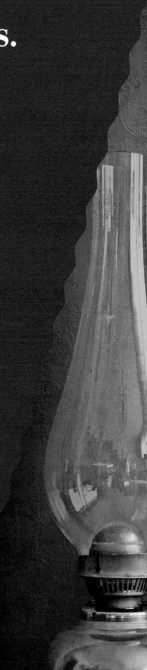

They left quickly.
Bread they made
could not rise.

We remember this.
How? We eat matzah.
It is a flat bread.

11

We share a meal.
It is called a seder.
Who comes?
Family. Friends.

Mom puts out a plate.

Look! It has six foods.

Each one is special.

Ann has soup.
What is in it?
Matzah balls.
Yum!

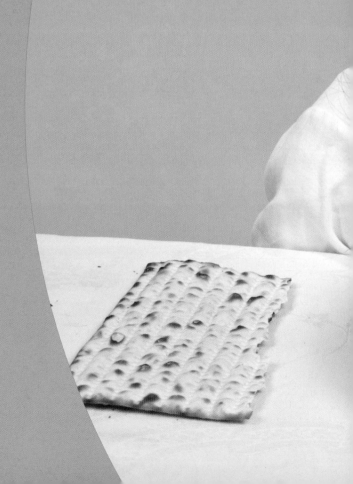

matzah
balls

Dad says a blessing.

He reads from
a book.

18

It has stories.

It has songs.

We sing.

We eat.

Happy Passover!

Symbols of Passover Seder

egg
An egg stands for a special offering Jews made on holidays.

horseradish
A bitter plant reminds Jews of the hard times in Egypt.

lamb bone
The Jews killed a lamb when they left Egypt.

sweet paste
This fruit and nut mix symbolizes the mortar the Jews used to build pyramids.

parsley
A vegetable is dipped in salt water, symbolizing the tears Jews cried as slaves.

romaine lettuce
A second bitter plant serves as another reminder of the hard times in Egypt.

Picture Glossary

Egypt
A country in
North Africa.

seder
The dinner
that Jews eat
on the first one
or two nights
of Passover.

Jew
A follower
of the religion
of Judaism;
Jews believe
in one God.

slaves
People who are
forced to work for
another person.

Index

To Learn More

Learning more is as easy as 1, 2, 3.

1) Go to www.factsurfer.com

2) Enter "Passover" into the search box.

3) Click the "Surf" button to see a list of websites.

With factsurfer.com, finding more information is just a click away.